5 Step Handbook

to a

Superior Customer Service Mindset

Five basic steps for anyone serious about excelling at customer service

by Sara Haggett

5 Step Handbook

to a Superior Customer Service Mindset

*Five basic steps for anyone serious about
excelling in customer service*

by Sara Haggett

https://sarahaggett.wixsite.com/website

Copyright ©2017 Sara Haggett

ISBN-13: 978-1544172071

ISBN-10: 1544172079

Printed in The United States of America.

Table of Contents

Chapter 1
Step One – Manners

As a child at the age of seven, I remember my parents holding many parties at their home. They had always thrown the most beautiful parties. I remember in the 80's on one occasion walking with the mayor at that time, giving him a tour of my family's home. As I walked with him I could have spoken about anything; the beautiful Italian Cypress trees that lined the perimeter of the walk way, or the aroma from the beautiful rose garden. I could have elaborated on the details about the unique neighborhood located at Stellar Air Park in Chandler, Arizona. Stellar is known for its private airport for the small neighborhood and the residence private aircrafts. I could have elaborated on my father's airplane or the beautiful flights on which he had taken us. As you can imagine the list goes on and on, with such energetic and adventurous parents there was quite a bit to discuss. Instead, as a seven-year-old, I chose to complain about all the work I had done for the party. I was walking with him around such a beautiful ambiance and telling him about all the cleaning and organizing I had done. In retrospect, for him listening and hanging on every word I said was so patient of him. When the tour was complete, the Mayor went straight to the kitchen to find my mother. He proceeded to review all my hard work with her. They both laughed and were quite amused. To this day, I keep reminding myself that I was just a child and my manners had not yet been refined. If this behavior were performed by an adult, it certainly would have been unacceptable.

I'm grateful for my parents spending the time to impress good manners and teach me that being right is not always right. This is a hard lesson to swallow even to this day. As I have worked for over twenty years in industries with clients, customers and patients, it became clear that parents are no longer taking the time to teach their kids very basic manners and concepts.

Without delay, below is a list of ten very basic manners that everyone should have mastered and be able to apply. You must practice refining and expanding your manners as an adult. Society is a much happier place when people use proper manners. Everyone can communicate and understand each other in a positive and supportive ways. Please make sure you have the following ten basic manners mastered. Use them regularly and with everyone.

Ten Basic Manners

1. Please, Thank You and You're Welcome
   a. Any time you ask for anything you need to include the word "Please".
   b. Anytime anything is done for you or given to you, you need to say "Thank you".
   c. When someone thanks you, you need to say "You're Welcome".
   Please remember:
   Your = belongs to you
   You're = you are
   Choose wisely when responding in writing.

2. Do not interrupt
   a. Listen when people are speaking to you, even if they are repeating themselves. People want to feel heard. If you must interrupt, please make sure to say "Excuse Me".

3. Ask permission first!
   a. Currently there are very few formalities in day-to-day societal behaviors. However, if you are in an unfamiliar

environment and you are unsure of proper etiquette, you must ask. Be mature and ask, and not at the time you are supposed to be delivering the edict, do so beforehand. Plan as much as possible for any situation you may be placed in.

4. If you don't have anything nice to say, do not say anything at all.

    a. Never make fun of people, and never say mean things about others.
    b. Keep all comments positive. Do not make negative comments.
    c. Never comment negatively or inquisitively on others' physical characteristics.

5. When people ask how you are or any question for that matter, you should respond and ask them the same questions.

6. When you have spent others time, thank them for that time. Time is money!

7. Door manners: Knock before entering. Always look behind you when walking through a door to hold it for the person behind you; man, woman or child.

8. When making a call, introduce yourself and then ask for the individual with whom you would like to speak.

9. If you see another working on something, ask them if they need help. Should anyone help you, make sure to say, "Thank you for your help."

10. Hygiene – Clean your body before leaving your home. Use any form of deodorant that works well for you when working with the public. Brush your teeth. Cover your mouth and/or nose when you cough or sneeze. Never cough or sneeze into a phone receiver, or in the direction of food or people. If you have nowhere to aim, aim down toward your body. Always cover the receiver and turn your head away from the receiver into the bend of your elbow. Table manners are also important hygiene manners. Chew your food with your mouth closed. Do not eat while speaking in a work

environment. Check your teeth after
you have eaten.

The above are extremely basic manners that everyone should have absolutely mastered before they move on to the second step to a superior customer service mindset. Manners need to be refined and expanded on. They are a constant study for each environment you enter. Use these manners with everyone, and not just when you are in a formal public setting. These extremely basic manners need to be part of you. These basic manners go a long way with family, friends, coworkers and especially customers. You will find that they will start using their manners too. You can help make the world a better place.

Once you have mastered your manners, you are one step closer to accomplishing a superior customer service mindset.

Chapter Two
Step Two – Ego

When I was sixteen my father gave me a Ford F-250, extended cab, long bed truck to drive. This truck was amazing, and it could hold all my friends in it. It was my first vehicle, and it was manual (stick shift). At the time, I lived in Kirkland, Washington. If you are familiar with Kirkland, you will know that every turn is a new hill. I became very good at driving a manual out of the pure fear of being stopped at a light on a hill and needing to go on a green. I would hold my breath and pray that I would not roll into the person behind me. It is very safe to say that I drove that truck like a race car after mastering the manual transmission. Now that I am much older, I thank God, my father did not get me a fast car. I would without a doubt be six feet under. Most of the time I would just coast into parking lots off the main road and swoop into a parking spot. At sixteen years old and a height of 5'5, I was just barely able to see over the steering wheel. People could barely see me driving the vehicle. After school I ran the video rental department at a local grocery store. I would drive into work with my huge truck coasting into the same parking spot as always. That truck just floated on in. I would pop it into granny gear, kill the engine and jump out. One day after work my manager walked me out. He said, "Sara, I have to tell you, a customer complained to me about your driving. She said that you were driving way too fast past the front entry doors, and she was scared someone would get hurt." I laughed dramatically, and told my manager that I was not driving fast and that the customer was for sure crazy." As I look back, I was driving way too fast. It was so kind of my manager to present it to me so nicely. I now see that instead of my priorities being focused on representing the business and the customers' concerns, it was all about me and how I thought the customer was so mean for saying something like that about me. However, it was not about me at all, rather about the customer and the business. I went home so upset, thinking how my manager could waste my time on this and why would he ever take the customer's word over mine. I was furious. Once I relaxed and remembered being right is not always right, I thought of how to rectify the situation with my manager. I approached him the next day and said, "Thank you for letting me know how the customer felt, and I will make an effort to slow down and try not to enter or exit in front of the main doors." He seemed relieved with this and I was back to super star status.

This is a perfect example of one's ego getting in the way at work. No matter how cool you think you are, how well you think you drive, who you are outside of work, you must remember that work is not about you and your ego! It is about the product and the company you are being paid to sell and promote. When people see you at work, you are representing the product, service and the company. Customers do not care or know how many social media friends or followers you have. They are going to your place of employment for themselves! This is all about them, NOT ABOUT YOU! Tell this to yourself about five times, and say it out loud so your brain and every cell in your body can hear it.

You must come to the basic realization that you are being paid for your **PERFORMANCE** at work. Whether you are the owner, manager or an employee, every person in a position that requires customer service is receiving money for a product or service being sold. If this were not the case, it would not be a business, and you might as well have stayed home, since you would most likely not be getting paid. It is very important to remember that the second you are seen in uniform or recognized by customers as an employee of a company, you are representing the product and services of the company for which you work by the customer.

It is imperative to remember you are getting "PAID" for your "PERFORMANCE". Your employer is reviewing your "PERFORMANCE". Most of the time, you go to the theater to see a performance because those in the performance are paid, professional "PERFORMERS"! You must realize that when you are at work, you are a paid professional performer, PERFORMING the job hired to do. In your mind, take a moment and imagine your job position. Image how you would envision someone in a movie or television show performing your job and performing it in the best possible manner the position could be performed. Write down what you are thinking and how you see it being performed. Most commonly, you would image someone focused, happy, energetically working, and accomplishing tasks quickly, correctly and independently. This is what an employee is paid for. Once again, for PERFORMANCE! If you wonder why you may have been skipped over for a promotion or a raise due to a performance review, you may need to visualize or watch another employee that is providing the PERFORMANCE that the business is looking for. Mirror that employee, and copy their exact words and expressions. You will eventually find your own voice to deliver the same information. The employee will be happy and flattered that you are listening to them and learning from them.

If you do not want to perform the job which is superior customer service, you should really reconsider your career path. You are wasting your time, and the company's time and money. You must have the intention of performing your job, including superior customer service.

Another step in dropping your ego is to have a sense of empowerment for the customer, not for yourself. If your customer comes in and says, "Hey, I just had the worst experience with your soda machine outside" or "with service received at the facility", the customer thinks you are the company, even if you are not the owner and are the lowest of seniority. They do not care about your title, they feel that they are complaining to the company when they are speaking to you. While using your basic manners, you need to have a sense of empowerment to write off their visit, or give them a soda for free off the shelf with a sincere, empathetic PERFORMANCE for their poor experience. No one is asking you to think twice about this issue after you clock out. It is important you impress on the customer that the company is taking their words and time seriously by doing something about it with an EMPATHETIC PERFORMANCE.

It is true, you sometimes must lose money to make money. Think about that situation. That customer will be coming back in to do business with the company for which you work based on your performance. That customer will tell their friends and family how happy they are with your facility, and that the company took great care of them. Not that you took great care of them, they will say the company did. You must understand a customer's worth. This is an example of that calculation. A customer is worth 1 visit per month which is equal to 12 visits a year. At $30 per visit this would equal $360.

$360 - $30(unsatisfactory visit) = $330

This would be the amount that customer contributes to the business and your salary. You must keep In mind the referrals that one person sends in is also an addition to this number.

This calculation is only if your customer leaves on great terms based on your PERFORMANCE and lack of EGO. If you have them pay for their unsatisfactory visit, and they leave with a feeling of loss, they won't come back and will probably tell people not to go to your facility. You will have received $30.00 total and no referrals. Each customer has a worth and it is not always what they end up paying at any one visit. Who knows they could bring in their soccer team or their employees to shop and experience the PERFORMANCE at the company.

TAKE OWNERSHIP! Think of it as your place and take care of business like it is your business. Image you are the owner and you are handling each customer personally. Always think what a good owner would do in any given situation.

To move on to step number three, to obtain a superior customer service mindset, you must master basic **manners**, leave your ego at home, and remember that you are getting **paid to put on a performance** as a professional representative of the company for which you work.

Chapter 3
Step Three
Intelligence/Emotional Intelligence

Some people are obsessed with thinking they must know the answer to everything or they think they sound unintelligent. With this mindset, they set themselves up for failure, becoming nervous, defensive, aggressive and ultimately becoming unapproachable to the point of pushing customers and colleagues away. This is a dangerous person to have in contact with customers. The customers are the ones bringing money into the business. This is someone who is not able to leave their ego out of it.

It is not about what information you know or how high your IQ is. It is about the words you choose to use to empower your customers and yourself. The key to making intelligent comments is the ability to **PLAN!** How do you PLAN? Use your emotional intelligence!

Emotional intelligence is the ability to understand and manage moods and emotions in one's self and in others. When using your emotional intelligence, you can read people by using your senses. You can visually see the customer. You can see their face. Is the customer smiling or frowning? Are they furrowing at the brow or are they crying? You can smell the customer; have they been drinking, smoking, not bathed or normal? You can hear the customer speaking or breathing. How is their tone? Do they sound out of breath? Do they sound like they need help? Are they angry? If you shake their hand, you can get a good idea if they are cold or hot, assertive or passive by the grip of their handshake. You can also see if they make eye contact while shaking your hand. This is a good indication of their sincerity, friendliness and intent.

By using the above emotional intelligence cues, it allows you to PLAN! This allows you to plan your response tone and your response speed. Be aware. If a patient looks very angry to be extra cautious. If the patient has been crying, apply some sympathy. Do not take it too far. No one is asking you to take them home and get involved with their problems. Do not jump right into their Sunday family dinner. Keep it professional.

Now, the intelligence part is broken down into two parts. First, employees are typically trained by someone. Don't take this time for granted. Whomever is training you is training you on the absolute must know how's. They have their own work to get back to. They are getting you up and going. Don't be mistaken, they are not training you on your manners or proper eye contact. Ask questions on who to escalate issues to and which departments handle what issues. Use this time to take very detailed notes. Take the notes home, type them up, print them out for the next day and make sure to ask questions on things you did not understand or have additional questions on. The second part of intelligence is planning the customer's visit and how their time will flow. Plan what words you are going to say. If you are aware that a certain customer comes every Thursday and asks you about the same issue every time, PLAN and have the answer ready for the customer. If you know the customer likes to have a certain item when in your facility, make sure it is ready and working. When the customer comes in, greet them and let them know you are ready for them, just supply what they need. Don't make a big deal about it, just do it so it's done. A great example of a follow-up with no resolution would be, "Welcome, I'm glad to see you. I wanted to let you know we still have not heard back regarding the issue we spoke about last time, and when I spoke with them today, they said they should know by a specific date". This will give the customer a lot of relief to know they were not forgotten and you are on top of it.

Intelligence comes from being proactive versus reactive. When you are caught off guard, you may say something that may not be accurate or may not sound very confident. Try not to say to a customer, "I don't know." If you don't know, you need to say, "Let me look into that for you and get back with you, I don't want to misinform you. What is the best number for me to contact you at?" Or you could say, "That is an interesting question. Let me call a [manager, billing department or the receiving clerk]." Unless you are all those titles, you may not be the best one to give them the most accurate information and the information may need to come from a specialty department. This is not because you are not intelligent, but because that is that department's specialty. Your specialty is your position and superior customer service! It is important to let the customer feel empowered.

Most customers also have the same intelligence complex. They want to sound intelligent and feel as though they are being heard and respected. You need to make sure you can make the customer feel heard, respected and valued. This is empowering the customer.

You also need to know how to recover from mistakes gracefully. Recovering from a mistake can go two ways. One, your ego gets in the way and you don't want to be wrong or admit fault. This makes for a very defensive and aggressive conversation. If you take responsibility for the mistake and disclose it with sincerity and regret in your tone for the minor error and how you plan to resolve it, the customer will again feel empowered and will feel more apt to forgive the company based on your sincerity. If they are upset, even after an authentic apology that you gave with authentic eye contact, then you need to say, "Let me get the manager." The manager will be proud of you in the end and the customer can only complain about the mistake, rather than your "Performance". Everyone makes mistakes, that's how you learn. How you handle the situation using your emotional intelligence and intelligence is what really matters.

Your words need to be positive. You can say anything with either a positive or negative attitude based on the words you choose. For example, a negative response to a customer trying to schedule an appointment would be, "We don't have anything open until Friday." A positive way to respond is by saying, with a positive tone, "We have an opening at 9am on

Friday, could I schedule you for that appointment time?" If you are speaking to customers, you need to choose to phrase things in a positive way. Another example, is if a patient is being seen by a doctor we don't say, "Did that hurt. I had that done and it hurt." Instead you would say, "I'm glad you came in today, we have seen so many people get better with this that same treatment, who have experienced similar symptoms as you. Thank you for coming in and we look forward to seeing you again." Or just say, "How was your visit today? Great! I'm so glad to hear that. We look forward to seeing you next time. Thank you. Your welcome."

Your greeting needs to be sincere and approachable. The way to do this is with your tone. Your voice will mirror your facial expression. Make sure your face appears happy or concerned, depending on your customer's demeanor. You need to be approachable, and this will lead to customers feeling comfortable asking questions and purchasing more from you. They will refer friends and family just on these basic steps that you need to be consistent with.

Now, being able to blend your **manners**, **performance you are performing**, **intelligence**

and emotional intelligence, you are well on your way and ready for step four to a superior customer service mindset.

Chapter 4
Communication

The first step to communication is listening! Again, drop the ego and take a moment to listen to what is being said. Use your training to think before responding. You should not find yourself saying, "What" after a customer askes you something. You need to work on your professional listening skills if you find yourself saying, "What". It is insulting to the customer and makes you look as though you are not interested and lazy. Having the customer repeat themselves is a poor performance.

Active listening takes practice. You need to listen carefully and remember what you hear. Most people cannot remember past seven items, and that's why phone numbers are seven digits. It is very important to always have a writing utensil and a piece of paper handy. I always recommend a spiral notebook so you can refer to it. You can look back throughout the day and ensure you followed up with everyone you said you would follow up with, or perform a task that was requested that may have fallen through the cracks on a busy day. While the person is speaking, write small notes. Start with the customer's name. Use the customer's name as much as possible throughout the conversation. If they give you their last name and the customer sounds like your senior, please refer to them by their title and last name until allowed by them to acknowledge them by their first name. When you hear the details given to you, write down the basic ideas they are saying. Here is an example: Mr. Jones, yesterday, worked with Sam, Sam short-changed the customer. This is going to give you the pieces to communicate with intelligence and emotional intelligence. You are going to write these items down as they are speaking and then convey it back to them so they know you understand. If there is a misunderstanding or missing vital information, the customer will be prompted to respond to you with that information, and you will need to add to or correct your notes. Then repeat it back to them again in this manner, "Let me make sure I understand Mr. Jones, you spoke with Sam yesterday who told you (..) and you believe you may have been short-changed. Am I understanding you correctly?" First, acknowledge the concern and apologize sincerely for their loss of time dealing with this matter. Ask the customer if they would mind if you researched this with the manager or with billing and if you could please either place them on hold or call them back. You can say that you do not want to keep them on hold for an excessive amount of time while you research the answer, and ask if there is any way you could get the information and call them back. Set up a cross check system to make sure by the end of your shift you have contacted that customer back. Even if you have no new information to give them, at least inform them on the plan for tomorrow or the next employee's shift and who else, besides yourself, maybe contacting them. This helps to build and rebuild relationships with the customers.

Do not use slang. A lot of times employees again get their EGO involved. This is strictly about your PERFORMANCE, not reliving your high school persona or your Mr. or Mrs. popularity contest with a too cool for school attitude. This is a PERFORMANCE representing the company by using complete sentences with proper language. "Ya" is not appropriate for the word yes. "Yes", "Please" or "No thank you" are basic forms of complete and proper communication. Always add positive adjectives. Get a thesaurus and know different meanings for the same word. For example, you could say, "It is wonderful to see you today," or "I am thrilled to see you today." If the customer says they had a good visit, you need to be excited about that comment as if you were the owner and it was your only customer. You need to use words such as; "Excellent to hear!", "I am so happy to hear that!", "That is phenomenal!" or "Perfect!" Your greetings and farewells need to be as sincere as possible. You need to make eye contact, exert energy and make sure your facial expression has a smile and is approachable. With those two in place, this is when you are going to say your greeting. "Welcome, how can I help you today? Never just say, "How can I help you?" You need to remember your basic manners. This is the same when someone is departing, you need to make eye contact with them and thank them for coming in, as well as welcome them back with a warm, sincere and approachable demeanor. Always, use the customer's name when the opportunity presents itself. After you have greeted your customer, you need to determine the needs of that customer. This is where your emotional intelligence/intelligence will come into play on how to respond next. If you have planned, you may know how and what to do with the customer. If it is a walk in, you will need to again take notes if they are telling you an issue. If not then be graceful and anticipate the need. This is your chance to make an imprint on the customer to remember the experience in a positive light! Above and beyond is your goal! You need to speak slowly in a clear, energetic and positive tone.

When you are speaking on the phone, you need to speak more slowly and pronounce your words clearly by opening your mouth wide to pronounce the words in a positive tone. Since the person cannot see you on the phone, they are relying on the tone of your voice to determine your attitude. If you are not performing, then your tone is going to be off, and you will sound rude and unwelcoming. You also need to remember all your manners, especially if you must place the customer on hold. You need to always ask; "May I please place you on hold for a moment?" Always wait for a response before placing them on hold. Then say, "Thank you, I will be just a moment." If it sounds like an emergency, take the call. However, even if you are on the phone, you need to visually acknowledge individuals coming in or leaving and tell them with your eyes, smile and wave hello or goodbye. The person on the phone may or may not come in to the business, however, the person in the office now is spending time and money and that needs to be respected and attended to first.

On their way out you should say, "How was your visit today?" It gives the customer the empowerment to inform you that it went great or something needs improvement. Either way you win. You can make the improvement and make them happy or they leave happy and you get to say, "I'm so happy to hear that." With a smile "Thank you for coming in, we look forward to seeing you again." We always want the customer to feel comfortable to express their wishes, no matter how big or small they seem.

Make sure if the customer starts speaking about something controversial (politics or religion) you gracefully change the subject without giving your opinion. What you say represents the company. The company may not agree with promoting a political or religious affiliation.

Once you have practiced and feel confident with this step, read on through to chapter five the final step to a superior customer service mindset.

Chapter 5
Non-Verbal Communication

After four years of working in a corporate environment as a staffing specialist, I was ready for a change. My office was located in the tallest building on the west coast, named the Columbia Tower, located in Seattle, Washington. I was done with having to drive to a Park and Ride, take a bus into the city, walk up multiple hills in business casual attire, all in the constant drizzle of the Seattle climate. It did not end there, once finally reaching the base of the building there were grandeur steps to get into the building and then finally to the elevators. To get to my office, I had to take two different sets of elevators with everyone else who was starting their shift at 7:00am. I was ready to work where I could drive up, park my car and walk in. So, I moved down to Buckeye, Arizona. I was fortunate that the manager of a Chiropractic office was moving across the country, so an opening had come up for me. On my first day, I can remember being very nervous that I was not sure that I would look the part for my performance. I did not have much medical background. When I pulled into a parking spot, parked and walked fifteen feet to the front door, I couldn't contain my sense of joy. Thinking that I was so happy already and this job met all my expectations, what could possibly happen? I was then greeted by an employee. I was mortified for the business when I saw this employee. My smile quickly changed into a look of shock. She was wearing a very high midriff shirt, extremely tight and low sitting jeans to where I could see her hip bones and almost her pelvis, with four-inch platform sandals. I was in shock. This was not appropriate to be representing a business and services offered. There was an immediate dress code change to scrubs and close toed active wear shoes.

The employee dressed inappropriately made these decisions based on her ego, rather than based on her professional performance. She must have thought it was a high school musical but instead it was a place of employment where she was getting paid to perform a professional job. If twelve years later I am still traumatized by that experience, imagine a customer and how they felt or reacted to a half-dressed woman helping them with therapy or coming in to get seen for the first time for massage therapy. There is a lack of trust for people who cannot dress themselves sensibly for work.

Let's face it, consumers almost always judge cleanliness, professionalism in employee appearance, professional employee behaviors and professionalism in employee communication. Again, they are judging the company's PERFORMANCE based on your performance. When you are dressed properly, you are more comfortable and are not worrying or concerned with garments. You also appear more confident. Sit, stand and walk professionally. Your performance in sitting, standing and walking needs to be deliberate. You would not be sitting on one leg hunched over your desk. You would appear ill or lazy. You need to sit up straight with both feet on the floor, unless you have a health issue that prevents this. When you are standing, and speaking with people, make sure you are using the proper distance and volume to speak. Also, always be aware that your facial expression is approachable and welcoming. You need to be aware of your surroundings and ensure that you are not blocking the flow or blocking other customers. Body language is very telling from both parties. This primarily begins with eye contact. A lack of eye contact creates a lack of trust. Always remember this, for if you are not able to make eye contact, you appear untrustworthy and unapproachable. If you are not smiling, your eyes will appear mean and unwelcoming. This is an important reason to smile besides the fact that this is a major part of your Superior Customer Service performance. Your face delivers a message. Your shoulders should be held up and not hunched over. When your shoulders are hunched over, it delivers the appearance of laziness. This does not convey much trust in your ability to help them or to follow through with their needs. Do not cross your arms and never have your hands in your pockets at work. Crossing your arms makes for an unapproachable, almost a hostile demeanor. When you place your hands in your pockets, it shows that you're not willing to be hands-on and you appear very lazy, not only to your employer but especially to customers. When you shake hands with men or women, it is important as a representative of the company to perform as though you are the owner meeting with a client. Make sure you make eye contact throughout the handshake and shake hands with a confident handshake. Please do not shake hands like a wet noodle hand. No one enjoys that and it really does not instill trust. This is again your PERFORMANCE!

"Never under estimate the power of body language."

~Ursula Sea Witch

Chapter 6
Tie It All Together

A common misconception is that people think they must be born with a charismatic performance. I do not believe that to be true. Just like learning a new language, you must practice and live all five steps. If you don't use this mindset, you will lose it! All five skills that you are refining will groom you for your charismatic performance that is in everyone. You must practice until you make it so. When I say, charismatic, I do not want it to be confused with flamboyant. In the beginning, you may not sound as natural as you would like, however as the experiences continue, you will refine your charismatic performance to fit your inner voice.

Practice by making scripts that are very professional. You may not feel comfortable saying them at first, but the customer will not know you are not comfortable. Please keep repeating phrases out loud, and eventually it will become natural. Refining and developing the five steps above will get you to a natural, charismatic performance. These are the five steps to a superior customer service mindset that are essential keys to provide your customers with a Superior Customer Service experience.

Magnetism and charm are the qualities of a charismatic performance. Let's talk about how we feel when we are around a truly charismatic performer who creates magnetism and charm. When we are around charismatic people, we feel love, joy, sincerity, honesty, integrity, commitment and most importantly, trust. Everyone wants to follow charismatic performers, and people are drawn to this positive energy. If you refine your charismatic performance, people will "look forward to" and "want to" come to your business, instead of the "need to" or "have to" go to your business. Customers will want to share the wonderful feeling listed above with friends and family. It's a wonderful way to see huge growth in your business and relationships with customers.

It is up to you to apply the information in this book! Read this handbook over and over. You will recognize something new to work on each time.

Thank you for taking the time to read this book and for applying these five steps. By doing so, **you are making the world in which we live a better place.**